CIRRHOSIS VEGAN DIET COOKBOOK FOR MEN

A Simple And Delicious Easy To Prepare Recipes To Help You

Joseph Robinson

INTRODUCTION

Welcome to the world of Cirrhosis Vegan Diet cooking! This cookbook is your guide to creating delicious, healthy, and healing plant-based meals to help improve your overall health and well-being.

Cirrhosis is a type of liver disease, and it affects millions of people around the world. The liver is a vital organ responsible for many of the body's functions, and when it is damaged by cirrhosis, it can put the person at risk for other health problems. Fortunately, there are steps you can take to protect your liver and improve your health.

One of the most important steps is to follow a cirrhosis vegan diet. This diet eliminates all animal products, including meat, dairy, and eggs, and focuses on plant-based foods. Eating a vegan diet can reduce inflammation, improve digestion, and may even help to repair liver damage.

This cookbook is designed to help you transition to a vegan diet for cirrhosis. We provide a wide range of recipes for breakfast, lunch, and dinner, as well as snacks and desserts. Each recipe has been carefully crafted to provide the nutrients you need to help improve your health.

I hope this cookbook will help you create delicious and nutritious meals that nourish your body and soul. With our help, you can make the transition to a cirrhosis vegan diet and enjoy better health and well-being.

CHAPTER ONE

Benefits of a Vegan Diet for Cirrhosis

Vegan diets have been gaining popularity in recent years due to their many health benefits. One of the most significant benefits of a vegan diet is the potential to reduce the risk of cirrhosis, a serious and potentially fatal liver disease. In this book, we will discuss the benefits of a vegan diet for cirrhosis, and how it may help reduce the risk of the condition. Cirrhosis is a serious condition that occurs when the liver is damaged or scarred. It is caused by long-term damage to the liver, often due to excessive alcohol consumption, chronic viral hepatitis, or other causes. Cirrhosis can lead to a wide range of serious health problems, including liver cancer, liver failure, and death.

There is evidence to suggest that following a vegan diet may reduce the risk of cirrhosis. One study found that following a vegan diet was associated with a lower risk of cirrhosis, compared to those who consumed a more traditional Western diet. This is likely due to the fact that vegan diets are typically low in saturated fat, and high in fiber. Additionally, vegan diets tend to be higher in antioxidants, which can help reduce inflammation that can lead to cirrhosis.

In addition to reducing the risk of cirrhosis, a vegan diet may also help improve overall liver health. A vegan diet is typically high in fiber, which can help to slow the absorption of fat in the liver. Additionally, vegan diets are typically low in saturated fat, which can help to reduce the amount of fat in the liver and reduce the risk of fatty liver disease. Furthermore, vegan diets are typically high in antioxidants, which can help reduce inflammation and improve liver health.

Finally, a vegan diet can also help to reduce the risk of other chronic diseases, such as heart disease and type 2 diabetes. This is due to the fact that vegan diets are typically high in fiber and low in saturated fat. Additionally, vegan diets are typically high in antioxidants, which can help reduce inflammation and improve overall health.

Overall, there is evidence to suggest that following a vegan diet may reduce the risk of cirrhosis. Additionally, it may help improve overall liver health, reduce the risk of other chronic diseases, and improve overall health. For those looking to reduce their risk of cirrhosis, a vegan diet may be a beneficial choice and this is because it is typically low in saturated fat and high in fiber and antioxidants. Although following a vegan diet may have many health benefits, it is important to speak to a healthcare professional before making any major changes to your diet. Additionally, it is important to ensure that a vegan diet is balanced and includes a variety of fruits, vegetables, proteins, and other essential nutrients as this will help to ensure that you are getting the proper nutrition. other benefits include weight loss and lower cholesterol levels. there are also side effects to consider such as vitamin B12 deficiency and iron deficiency.

CHAPTER TWO

Basic Principles Of A Cirrhosis Vegan Diet

A cirrhosis vegan diet is one of the best ways to prevent and manage cirrhosis and its associated symptoms. This type of diet is based on the principles of a vegan diet, which focuses on consuming only plant-based foods. This type of diet is recommended for individuals with cirrhosis, as it can help reduce symptoms, improve overall health, and reduce the risk of cirrhosis-related complications.

The basic principles of a cirrhosis vegan diet include:

1. Eating more plant-based foods: Plant-based foods are rich in vitamins, minerals, antioxidants, and other important nutrients. They also help reduce inflammation and improve overall health. Examples of plant-based foods include fruits, vegetables, legumes, whole grains, nuts, and seeds.

2. Avoiding processed foods: Processed foods contain added sugar, salt, and unhealthy fats. These can increase inflammation and worsen cirrhosis-related symptoms.

3. Eating more fiber: Fiber helps to keep the digestive tract healthy and can reduce the risk of complications associated with cirrhosis. High-fiber foods should be included in a cirrhosis vegan diet, such as whole grains, fruits, vegetables, nuts, and seeds.

4. Consuming more antioxidants: Antioxidants are important for reducing inflammation and preventing oxidative damage to cells.

Foods high in antioxidants include dark, leafy greens, fruits, nuts, and seeds.

5. Eating more plant-based proteins: Plant-based proteins are important for maintaining muscle mass and keeping the body healthy. Other very good sources include legumes, nuts, and seeds.

6. Limiting saturated fats: Saturated fats should be limited in a cirrhosis vegan diet, as these can worsen cirrhosis-related symptoms. Instead, opt for unsaturated fats found in foods such as avocados, nuts, and seeds.

7. Avoiding alcohol: Alcohol can worsen cirrhosis symptoms and increase the risk of complications. It should be avoided in a cirrhosis vegan diet.

8. Eating regularly: Eating regular meals and snacks is important for maintaining a healthy weight and keeping the body nourished.

9. Drinking plenty of water: Drinking plenty of water helps to keep the digestive tract healthy and reduces the risk of dehydration.

10. Taking supplements: In some cases, supplements may be necessary to ensure that all essential nutrients are consumed. Speak to a doctor or dietitian before taking any supplements.

11. Avoiding high-sodium foods: High-sodium foods can worsen cirrhosis-related symptoms and should be avoided.

12. Avoiding high-fat foods: High-fat foods can increase inflammation and worsen cirrhosis-related symptoms.

13. Eating foods with a low glycemic index: Foods with a low glycemic index can help to maintain a healthy weight and reduce the risk of complications associated with cirrhosis.

14. Limiting caffeine: Caffeine can increase inflammation and worsen cirrhosis-related symptoms. Therefore, it should be limited to a cirrhosis vegan diet.

15. Eating foods with a low purine content: Foods with a high purine content can increase the risk of complications associated with cirrhosis. Low-purine foods include fruits, vegetables, and legumes.

16. Eating foods rich in essential fatty acids: Essential fatty acids are important for maintaining a healthy weight and reducing inflammation. Foods rich in essential fatty acids include flaxseeds, chia seeds, and walnuts.

17. Avoiding refined sugars: Refined sugars can worsen cirrhosis-related symptoms and should be avoided.

18. Eating foods rich in iron: Iron-rich foods are important for maintaining energy levels and preventing anemia. Very beneficial sources include legumes, nuts, and seeds.

19. Consuming probiotics: Probiotics are beneficial bacteria that can help reduce inflammation and improve overall health. Some fermented foods, such as yogurt and kefir also contains Probiotics

20. Avoiding processed meats: Processed meats should be avoided in a cirrhosis vegan diet, as these can worsen cirrhosis-related symptoms.

CHAPTER THREE

Recipes For Breakfast

1. Banana Oatmeal Pancakes – Preparation: 15 minutes, Cooking Time: 15 minutes

Ingredients: 1 cup of oatmeal, 1 banana, 1 teaspoon of baking powder, 1 tablespoon of brown sugar, 1 tablespoon of vegetable oil, and 1 cup of almond milk.

Instructions:

1. In a large bowl, mash the banana with a fork until it is mostly smooth.

2. Add in the oatmeal, baking powder, brown sugar, vegetable oil, and almond milk. To create a thick batter, combine all ingredients.

3. A nonstick skillet should be heated to medium.

4. Grease the skillet with a little extra oil if needed.

5. Ladle the batter onto the skillet, making sure to leave enough room between each pancake.

6. Cook for 2-3 minutes on each side, or until golden brown.

7. Serve with your favorite toppings.

2. Tofu French Toast – Preparation: 10 minutes, Cooking Time: 10 minutes

Ingredients: 1 block of firm tofu, 2 tablespoons of vegan milk, 2 tablespoons of maple syrup, 2 tablespoons of nutritional yeast, 1 teaspoon of ground cinnamon, and 2 tablespoons of coconut oil.

Instructions:

1. In a shallow bowl, mash the tofu with a fork until it is mostly smooth.

2. Add in the vegan milk, maple syrup, nutritional yeast, and cinnamon. To create a thick batter, combine all ingredients.

3. Set a nonstick frying pan to medium heat.

4. Grease the skillet with coconut oil.

5. Dip the bread slices into the batter, making sure to coat evenly.

6. Place the dipped slices onto the skillet.

7. Cook for 2-3 minutes on each side, or until golden brown.

8. Serve with your favorite toppings.

3. Overnight Oats – Preparation: 10 minutes, Cooking Time: Overnight

Ingredients: 1 cup of rolled oats, 2 tablespoons of chia seeds, 1 tablespoon of maple syrup, 1 teaspoon of ground cinnamon, 1 cup of almond milk, 1/4 cup of chopped walnuts, 1/4 cup of dried cranberries, 1/4 cup of vegan yogurt.

Instructions:

1. In a bowl, combine the rolled oats, chia seeds, maple syrup, and cinnamon.

2. Pour in the almond milk and stir until everything is combined.

3. Add in the walnuts and cranberries.

4. Transfer the mixture to a mason jar or other airtight container.

5. Refrigerate overnight.

6. In the morning, add in the vegan yogurt and stir until everything is combined.

7. Serve with your favorite toppings.

4. Vegan Breakfast Burrito – Preparation: 15 minutes, Cooking Time: 15 minutes

Ingredients: 1/2 cup of cooked black beans, 1/2 cup of cooked quinoa, 1/2 cup of cooked sweet potato, 1/4 cup of chopped bell pepper, 1/4 cup of chopped onion, 1/4 cup of chopped spinach, 1/4 cup of salsa, 1/4 teaspoon of ground cumin, 1/4 teaspoon of ground coriander, 2 tablespoons of olive oil, 4 large tortillas.

Instructions:

1. Over medium heat, warm the olive oil in a large skillet.

2. Add in the bell pepper, onion, and spinach. Sauté until the vegetables are softened.

3. Add in the cooked black beans, quinoa, and sweet potato.

4. Sprinkle in the cumin and coriander.

5. Cook for 5-7 minutes, or until everything is heated through.

6. Heat the tortillas in the microwave for 30 seconds, or until softened.

7. Place the filling onto the center of each tortilla.

8. Fold the sides of the tortilla inwards, then roll it up tightly.

9. Serve with salsa.

5. Baked Sweet Potato Hash – Preparation: 10 minutes, Cooking Time: 30 minutes

Ingredients: 2 large sweet potatoes, 1/2 cup of chopped red onion, 1/2 cup of diced bell pepper, 1/4 cup of chopped mushrooms, 1/4 cup of chopped kale, 1 tablespoon of olive oil, 1 teaspoon of garlic powder, 1 teaspoon of paprika, 1/2 teaspoon of ground cumin, 1/4 teaspoon of sea salt.

Instructions:

1. Preheat the oven to 400°F.

2. Peel and cube the sweet potatoes.

3. In a large bowl, combine the sweet potatoes, red onion, bell pepper, mushrooms, kale, olive oil, garlic powder, paprika, cumin, and salt.

4. Spread the mixture onto a baking sheet.

5. Bake for 30 minutes, or until the sweet potatoes are tender.

6. Serve with your favorite toppings.

6. Savory Breakfast Muffins – Preparation: 10 minutes, Cooking Time: 25 minutes

Ingredients: 1 cup of all-purpose flour, 1/2 cup of rolled oats, 1 teaspoon of baking powder, 1 teaspoon of garlic powder, 1/2 teaspoon of sea salt, 1/4 teaspoon of ground black pepper, 1/2 cup of vegan milk, 1 tablespoon of olive oil, 1/4 cup of cooked quinoa, 1/4 cup of chopped spinach, 1/4 cup of chopped mushrooms, 1/4 cup of chopped bell pepper.

Instructions:

1. Preheat the oven to 375°F.

2. Use a little olive oil to grease a muffin pan.

3. Combine the flour, oats, baking soda, garlic powder, salt, and pepper in a big bowl.

4. Add the olive oil and vegan milk. To create a thick batter, combine all ingredients.

5. Include the bell pepper, mushrooms, quinoa, and spinach. Stir everything together thoroughly.

6. Pour the batter into the muffin tin that has been ready.

7. Bake the muffins for 25 minutes, or until golden brown.

8. Serve warm.

7. Avocado Toast – Preparation: 5 minutes, Cooking Time: 5 minutes

Ingredients: 2 slices of whole grain bread, 1 ripe avocado, 1/4 teaspoon of sea salt, 1/4 teaspoon of ground black pepper, 1/2 teaspoon of garlic powder, 1/2 teaspoon of red pepper flakes, 1 tablespoon of olive oil.

Instructions:

1. Toast the bread in a toaster or under the broiler in the oven.

2. In a small bowl, mash the avocado with a fork until it is mostly smooth.

3. Add in the salt, pepper, garlic powder, and red pepper flakes. Mix together until everything is combined.

4. Spread the avocado mixture onto the toast slices.

5. Drizzle with olive oil.

6. Serve immediately.

8. Veggie Omelette – Preparation: 10 minutes, Cooking Time: 10 minutes

Ingredients: 2 tablespoons of olive oil, 1/4 cup of chopped bell pepper, 1/4 cup of chopped mushrooms, 1/4 cup of chopped spinach, 1/4 cup of vegan cheese, 1/4 teaspoon of sea salt, 1/4 teaspoon of ground black pepper, 4 large eggs.

Instructions:

1. In a big skillet over medium heat, warm the olive oil.

2. Include the spinach, mushrooms, and bell pepper. Sauté the vegetables until they are tender.

3. Include the vegan cheese and add salt and pepper to taste.

4. In a bowl, combine the eggs and whisk them until they are frothy and light.

5. Transfer the egg mixture to the pan.

6. Cook for 5-7 minutes, or until the egg is cooked through and the cheese is melted.

7. Serve with your favorite toppings.

9. Fruit and Nut Granola – Preparation: 10 minutes, Cooking Time: 25 minutes

Ingredients: 2 cups of rolled oats, 1/4 cup of chopped walnuts, 1/4 cup of chopped almonds, 1/4 cup of chopped pecans, 2 tablespoons of flax seed, 2 tablespoons of chia seed, 2 tablespoons of maple syrup, 2 tablespoons of coconut oil, 1/4 cup of dried cranberries, 1/4 cup of dried cherries.

Instructions:

1. Preheat the oven to 350°F.

2. In a bowl, combine the rolled oats, walnuts, almonds, pecans, flax seed, chia seed, maple syrup, and coconut oil.

3. Evenly distribute the mixture on a baking sheet.

4. Bake the granola for 25 minutes, or until golden brown.

5. Take the food out of the oven and let it cool.

6. Add in the dried cranberries and cherries.

7. Store the granola in an airtight container.

10. Tofu Scramble – Preparation: 10 minutes, Cooking Time: 10 minutes

Ingredients: 1 block of firm tofu, 1 tablespoon of olive oil, 1/4 cup of chopped onion, 1/4 cup of chopped bell pepper, 1/4 cup of chopped mushrooms, 1/4 teaspoon of sea salt, 1/4 teaspoon of ground black pepper, 1/2 teaspoon of garlic powder, 1/2 teaspoon of turmeric, 1/4 cup of vegan cheese.

Instructions:

1. In a big skillet over medium heat, warm the olive oil.

2. Add in the onion, bell pepper, and mushrooms. Sauté until the vegetables are softened.

3. Crumble the tofu into the skillet.

4. Sprinkle in the salt, pepper, garlic powder, and turmeric.

5. Cook for 5-7 minutes, or until the tofu is heated through and the vegetables are cooked.

6. Add in the vegan cheese and stir until melted.

7. Serve with your favorite toppings.

11. Banana Walnut Smoothie – Preparation: 5 minutes

Ingredients: 1 banana, 1 cup of almond milk, 2 tablespoons of rolled oats, 2 tablespoons of chopped walnuts, 2 tablespoons of vegan yogurt, 1 teaspoon of ground cinnamon, 1 tablespoon of honey.

Instructions:

1. Fill a blender with all the ingredients.

2. Blend until smooth.

3. Serve cold.

12. Acai Bowl – Preparation: 10 minutes

Ingredients: 1/2 cup of frozen acai berries, 1/2 cup of frozen blueberries, 1/2 cup of frozen banana, 1/2 cup of almond milk, 2 tablespoons of vegan yogurt, 2 tablespoons of rolled oats, 2 tablespoons of chopped walnuts, 2 tablespoons of coconut flakes, 1 teaspoon of ground cinnamon.

Instructions:

1. Add each ingredient to the blender.

2. Blend until smooth.

3. Pour the mixture into a bowl and top with your favorite toppings.

13. Green Smoothie Bowl – Preparation: 10 minutes

Ingredients: 1/2 cup of frozen spinach, 1/2 cup of frozen banana, 1/2 cup of almond milk, 2 tablespoons of vegan yogurt, 2 tablespoons of rolled oats, 2 tablespoons of chopped walnuts, 2 tablespoons of chia seed, 1 teaspoon of ground cinnamon.

Instructions:

In a blender, combine all the ingredients.

2. Blend until smooth.

3. Pour the mixture into a bowl and top with your favorite toppings.

14. Overnight Oats Parfait – Preparation: 10 minutes, Cooking Time: Overnight

Ingredients: 1 cup of rolled oats, 2 tablespoons of chia seeds, 1 tablespoon of maple syrup, 1 teaspoon of ground cinnamon, 1 cup of almond milk, 1/4 cup of chopped walnuts, 1/4 cup of dried cranberries, 1/4 cup of vegan yogurt, 1/4 cup of fresh berries.

Instructions:

1. In a bowl, combine the rolled oats, chia seeds, maple syrup, and cinnamon.

2. Pour in the almond milk and stir until everything is combined.

3. Add in the walnuts and cranberries.

4. Transfer the mixture to a mason jar or other airtight container.

5. Refrigerate overnight.

6. In the morning, layer the oats mixture with the vegan yogurt and fresh berries in a glass.

7. Serve with your favorite toppings.

15. Baked Sweet Potato Hash Browns – Preparation: 10 minutes, Cooking Time: 30 minutes

Ingredients: 2 large sweet potatoes, 1/4 cup of chopped onion, 1/4 cup of chopped bell pepper, 1/4 cup of chopped mushrooms, 1 tablespoon of olive oil, 1 teaspoon of garlic powder, 1/2 teaspoon of paprika, 1/4 teaspoon of sea salt.

Instructions:

1. Preheat the oven to 400°F.

2. Peel and grate the sweet potatoes.

3. In a large bowl, combine the grated sweet potato, onion, bell pepper, mushrooms, olive oil, garlic powder, paprika, and salt.

4. Spread the mixture onto a baking sheet.

5. Bake for 30 minutes, or until the hash browns are golden brown.

6. Serve with your favorite toppings.

16. Breakfast Burrito Bowl – Preparation: 10 minutes, Cooking Time: 10 minutes

Ingredients: 1/2 cup of cooked quinoa, 1/2 cup of cooked black beans, 1/2 cup of cooked sweet potato, 1/4 cup of chopped bell pepper, 1/4 cup of chopped onion, 1/4 cup of chopped spinach, 1/4 cup of salsa, 1/4 teaspoon of ground cumin, 1/4 teaspoon of ground coriander, 2 tablespoons of olive oil.

Instructions:

1. In a big skillet over medium heat, warm the olive oil.

2. Add in the bell pepper, onion, and spinach. Sauté until the vegetables are softened.

3. Add in the cooked quinoa, black beans, and sweet potato.

4. Sprinkle in the cumin and coriander.

5. Cook for 5-7 minutes, or until everything is heated through.

6. Serve in a bowl with salsa.

17. Vegan Breakfast Tacos – Preparation: 15 minutes, Cooking Time: 15 minutes

Ingredients: 1/2 cup of cooked black beans, 1/2 cup of cooked quinoa, 1/2 cup of cooked sweet potato, 1/4 cup of chopped bell pepper, 1/4 cup of chopped onion, 1/4 cup of chopped spinach, 1/4 cup of salsa, 1/4 teaspoon of ground cumin, 1/4 teaspoon of ground coriander, 2 tablespoons of olive oil, 4 small tortillas.

Instructions:

1. Put a big skillet on medium heat and add the olive oil.

2. Add in the bell pepper, onion, and spinach. Sauté until the vegetables are softened.

3. Add in the cooked black beans, quinoa, and sweet potato.

4. Sprinkle in the cumin and coriander.

5. Cook for 5-7 minutes, or until everything is heated through.

6. Heat the tortillas in the microwave for 30 seconds, or until softened.

7. Place the filling onto the center of each tortilla.

8. Fold the sides of the tortilla inwards and serve.

18. Chia Seed Pudding – Preparation: 10 minutes, Cooking Time: Overnight

Ingredients: 1/2 cup of chia seeds, 2 cups of almond milk, 2 tablespoons of maple syrup, 1 teaspoon of ground cinnamon, 1/4 cup of chopped walnuts, 1/4 cup of dried cranberries, 1/4 cup of vegan yogurt.

Instructions:

1. In a bowl, combine the chia seeds, almond milk, maple syrup, and cinnamon.

2. Stir until everything is combined.

3. Transfer the mixture to a mason jar or other airtight container.

4. Refrigerate overnight.

5. In the morning, layer the pudding with walnuts, cranberries, and vegan yogurt in a glass.

6. Serve with your favorite toppings.

19. Apple Cinnamon Oatmeal – Preparation: 10 minutes, Cooking Time: 10 minutes

Ingredients: 1 cup of rolled oats, 1 cup of almond milk, 1 small apple, peeled and diced, 1 teaspoon of ground cinnamon, 2 tablespoons of maple syrup, 1 tablespoon of vegan butter, 1/4 cup of chopped walnuts.

Instructions:

1. Heat the almond milk in a large saucepan over medium heat.

2. Add in the oats, apple, and cinnamon.

3. Cook for 5-7 minutes, stirring occasionally, until the oatmeal is thick and creamy.

4. Stir in the maple syrup and vegan butter.

5. Serve with walnuts and your favorite toppings.

20. Zucchini Fritters – Preparation: 10 minutes, Cooking Time: 15 minutes

Ingredients: 2 cups of grated zucchini, 1/4 cup of all-purpose flour, 1/4 cup of vegan milk, 1/2 teaspoon of sea salt, 1/2 teaspoon of ground black pepper, 1/4 teaspoon of garlic powder, 1/4 teaspoon of paprika, 1/4 cup of vegan cheese, 2 tablespoons of olive oil.

Instructions:

Grated zucchini, flour, vegan milk, salt, pepper, garlic powder, paprika, and vegan cheese should all be combined in a bowl. To create a thick batter, combine all ingredients.

2. In a big skillet over medium heat, warm the olive oil.

3. Spoon the batter into the skillet, making sure to leave enough room between each fritter.

4. Cook for 5-7 minutes on each side, or until golden brown.

5. Serve with your favorite toppings.

CHAPTER FOUR

Recipes For Lunch

1. Quinoa and Veggie Bowl - Preparation time: 10 minutes

Ingredients:

- 1 cup cooked quinoa

- 1 cup cooked vegetables of your choice (such as broccoli, carrots, bell pepper, mushrooms, etc.)

- 1/4 cup cooked beans of your choice (such as chickpeas, black beans, etc.)

- 1/4 cup diced avocado

- 2 tablespoons diced red onion

- 2 tablespoons chopped fresh cilantro

- 2 tablespoons extra-virgin olive oil

- 1 teaspoon freshly squeezed lime juice

- To taste, add salt and freshly ground black pepper.

Instructions:

1. Prepare the quinoa as directed on the package.

2. Prepare the desired veggies and beans in a different saucepan or the microwave.

3. Combine the cooked quinoa, beans, and vegetables in a big bowl.

4. Include the olive oil, lime juice, cilantro, red onion, and cubed avocado.

5. To taste, add salt and pepper to the food.

6. Toss the ingredients together until combined.

7. Serve warm or chilled.

2. Eggplant and Chickpea Curry - Preparation time: 15 minutes

Ingredients:

- 1 tablespoon olive oil

- 1 small onion, diced

- 1 garlic clove, minced

- 1 teaspoon ground cumin

- 1 teaspoon ground coriander

- 1/2 teaspoon ground turmeric

- 1/4 teaspoon ground cinnamon

- 1/4 teaspoon ground cardamom

- 1/2 teaspoon sea salt

- 1/4 teaspoon freshly ground black pepper

- 1 medium eggplant, diced

- One (15 oz) can of washed and drained chickpeas

- One 14.5 ounce can of chopped tomatoes

- A half-cup of vegetable broth

-2 teaspoons of just-chopped cilantro

Instructions:

1. In a big skillet over medium heat, warm the olive oil.

2. Add the onion and garlic and cook until softened, about 4 minutes.

3. Add the cumin, coriander, turmeric, cinnamon, cardamom, salt, and pepper and cook for 1 minute.

4. Add the eggplant and cook for 5 minutes.

5. Add the chickpeas, tomatoes, and vegetable broth and bring to a simmer.

6. Simmer for 10 minutes, stirring occasionally.

7. Add the cilantro and stir to combine.

8. Serve hot with cooked quinoa or other cooked grains.

3. Lentil and Zucchini Soup - Preparation time: 25 minutes

Ingredients:

- 1 tablespoon olive oil

- 1 onion, diced

- 2 cloves garlic, minced

- 1 teaspoon ground cumin

- 1/2 teaspoon ground coriander

- 1/2 teaspoon ground turmeric

- 1/2 teaspoon sea salt

- 1/4 teaspoon freshly ground black pepper

- 1 cup dried lentils, rinsed and drained

- 4 cups vegetable broth

- 2 medium zucchinis, diced

- 2 tablespoons freshly chopped parsley

Instructions:

1. In a big skillet over medium heat, warm the olive oil.

2. Add the onion and garlic and cook until softened, about 4 minutes.

3. Add the cumin, coriander, turmeric, salt, and pepper and cook for 1 minute.

4. Add the lentils and vegetable broth and bring to a simmer.

5. Simmer for 15 minutes, stirring occasionally.

6. Add the zucchini and cook for 5 more minutes.

7. Stir in the parsley and season with additional salt and pepper to taste.

8. Serve hot with a dollop of plain yogurt or other vegan yogurts.

4. Mushroom Risotto - Preparation time: 25 minutes

Ingredients:

- 2 tablespoons olive oil

- 1 onion, diced

- 2 cloves garlic, minced

- 8 ounces mushrooms, sliced

- 1 cup Arborio rice

- 4 cups vegetable broth

- 2 tablespoons freshly chopped parsley

- 1/4 cup freshly grated Parmesan cheese

Instructions:

1. In a big pot over medium heat, warm the olive oil.

2. Add the onion and garlic and simmer for 4 minutes or until tender.

3. Include the mushrooms and simmer for a further 4 minutes.

4. Include the Arborio rice and blend by stirring.

5. Include the veggie broth and boil for five minutes.

6. Simmer, stirring regularly, for 15 minutes.

7. Add the Parmesan cheese and parsley.

8. Serve hot.

5. Polenta and Black Bean Burrito Bowl - Preparation time: 15 minutes

Ingredients:

- 1 tablespoon olive oil

- 1 onion, diced

- 2 cloves garlic, minced

- 1 teaspoon ground cumin

- 1/2 teaspoon ground coriander

- 1/2 teaspoon chili powder

- 1/2 teaspoon sea salt

- 1/4 teaspoon freshly ground black pepper

- 1 cup cooked polenta

- 1 can (15 oz) rinsed and drained black beans

- One cup of cooked corn

-2 teaspoons of just-chopped cilantro

- One-fourth cup vegan sour cream

14 cup salsa

Instructions:

1. In a big skillet over medium heat, warm the olive oil.

2. Add the onion and garlic and cook until softened, about 4 minutes.

3. Add the cumin, coriander, chili powder, salt, and pepper and cook for 1 minute.

4. Add the polenta and cook for 5 minutes, stirring occasionally.

5. Add the black beans and corn and cook for 5 more minutes.

6. Stir in the cilantro.

7. To serve, divide the polenta and bean mixture among four bowls.

8. Top each bowl with a dollop of vegan sour cream and salsa.

6. Chickpea and Spinach Curry - Preparation time: 25 minutes

Ingredients:

- 2 tablespoons olive oil

- 1 onion, diced

- 2 cloves garlic, minced

- 1 teaspoon ground cumin

- 1 teaspoon ground coriander

- 1/2 teaspoon ground turmeric

- 1/2 teaspoon sea salt

- 1/4 teaspoon freshly ground black pepper

- One (15 oz) can of washed and drained chickpeas

- One 14.5 ounce can of chopped tomatoes

- A half-cup of vegetable broth

- 2 cups young spinach - 2 teaspoons finely chopped fresh cilantro

Instructions:

1. In a big skillet over medium heat, warm the olive oil.

2. Add the onion and garlic and cook until softened, about 4 minutes.

3. Add the cumin, coriander, turmeric, salt, and pepper and cook for 1 minute.

4. Add the chickpeas, tomatoes, and vegetable broth and bring to a simmer.

5. Simmer for 10 minutes, stirring occasionally.

6. Add the spinach and cook for 5 more minutes.

7. Stir in the cilantro and season with additional salt and pepper to taste.

8. Serve hot with cooked quinoa or other cooked grains.

7. Roasted Vegetable and Hummus Wrap - Preparation time: 15 minutes

Ingredients:

- 4 whole wheat wraps

- 2 cups cooked vegetables of your choice (such as Brussels sprouts, asparagus, bell peppers, mushrooms, etc.)

- 2 tablespoons olive oil- 1/2 teaspoon sea salt

- 1/4 teaspoon freshly ground black pepper

- 1/2 cup hummus

- 2 tablespoons freshly chopped parsley

Instructions:

1. Preheat the oven to 375°F (190°C).

2. Place the vegetables on a baking sheet and drizzle with the olive oil.

3. Sprinkle with salt and pepper.

4. Roast in the preheated oven for 10 minutes.

5. Spread the hummus onto each wrap.

6. Top each wrap with the roasted vegetables.

7. Sprinkle with the parsley.

8. Roll up the wraps and serve.

8. Lentil Tacos - Preparation time: 25 minutes

Ingredients:

- 2 tablespoons olive oil

- 1 onion, diced

- 2 cloves garlic, minced

- 1 teaspoon ground cumin

- 1/2 teaspoon ground coriander

- 1/2 teaspoon chili powder

- 1/2 teaspoon sea salt

- 1/4 teaspoon freshly ground black pepper

- 1 cup rinsed and drained dried lentils

14.5 ounces of diced tomatoes in a can; 1/2 cup of vegetable broth

- Eight little corn tortillas

- One-quarter cup freshly chopped cilantro

Instructions:

1. In a big skillet over medium heat, warm the olive oil.

2. Add the onion and garlic and cook until softened, about 4 minutes.

3. Add the cumin, coriander, chili powder, salt, and pepper and cook for 1 minute.

4. Add the lentils, tomatoes, and vegetable broth and bring to a simmer.

5. Simmer for 15 minutes, stirring occasionally.

6. Heat the tortillas in a separate pan or in the microwave.

7. To assemble the tacos, spoon the lentil mixture onto each tortilla and top with the cilantro.

8. Serve immediately.

9. Zucchini Noodles with Cashew Cream Sauce - Preparation time: 20 minutes

Ingredients:

- 2 tablespoons olive oil

- 1 onion, diced

- 2 cloves garlic, minced

- 1/2 teaspoon sea salt

- 1/4 teaspoon freshly ground black pepper

- 2 medium zucchinis, spiralized

- 1/2 cup raw cashews, soaked in water for 4 hours

- 1/2 cup vegetable broth

- 2 tablespoons freshly chopped parsley

Instructions:

1. In a big skillet over medium heat, warm the olive oil.

2. Add the onion and garlic and cook until softened, about 4 minutes.

3. Add the salt and pepper and cook for 1 minute.

4. Add the zucchini noodles and cook for 5 minutes.

5. Drain the cashews and place them in a blender or food processor.

6. Add the vegetable broth and blend until smooth.

7. Pour the cashew cream sauce over the zucchini noodles and stir to combine.

8. Sprinkle with the parsley and serve.

10. Marinated Tofu and Veggie Stir-Fry - Preparation time: 25 minutes

Ingredients:

- 1/4 cup tamari

- 2 tablespoons mirin

- 2 tablespoons sesame oil

- 1 tablespoon freshly grated ginger

- 1/2 teaspoon sea salt

- 1/4 teaspoon freshly ground black pepper

- 1/2 pound extra-firm tofu, drained and cubed

- 2 tablespoons olive oil

- 1 onion, diced

- 2 cloves garlic, minced

- 2 cups cooked vegetables of your choice (such as broccoli, carrots, bell pepper, mushrooms, etc.)

- 2 tablespoons freshly chopped cilantro

Instructions:

1. In a small bowl, whisk together the tamari, mirin, sesame oil, ginger, salt, and pepper.

2. Place the cubed tofu in a shallow dish and pour the marinade over top. Let marinate for 10 minutes.

3. In a big skillet over medium heat, warm the olive oil.

4. Add the onion and garlic and cook until softened, about 4 minutes.

5. Add the marinated tofu and cook for 5 minutes.

6. Add the cooked vegetables and cook for 5 more minutes.

7. Stir in the cilantro and season with additional salt and pepper to taste.

8. Serve hot.

11. Avocado Toast - Preparation time: 5 minutes

Ingredients:

- 2 slices whole wheat bread

- 1 ripe avocado

- 2 teaspoons freshly squeezed lemon juice

- 1/4 teaspoon sea salt

- 1/4 teaspoon freshly ground black pepper

Instructions:

1. Toast the bread slices in a toaster or in a skillet over medium heat.

2. Mash the avocado in a small bowl.

3. Add the lemon juice, salt, and pepper and mix until combined.

4. Spread the avocado mixture onto the toast slices.

5. Serve immediately.

12. Baked Falafel - Preparation time: 25 minutes

Ingredients:

- 1 can (15 oz) washed and drained chickpeas.

- Diced onion, one

- 2 minced cloves of garlic

- 1 teaspoon powdered cumin

- 1/2 teaspoon ground coriander

- 2 tablespoons freshly chopped parsley

- 1 teaspoon of ground cumin and 1/2 teaspoon of ground coriander

 - 2 tablespoons each of finely chopped parsley and cilantro;

- 2 tablespoons olive oil

Instructions:

1. Set the oven to 375°F (190°C) before using it.

2. Combine the chickpeas, salt, pepper, onion, garlic, parsley, cilantro, cumin, and other spices in a food processor.

3. Pulse the ingredients until they are blended but still slightly lumpy.

4. Place a large scoop of the mixture in a bowl, and then form it into 8 patties.

5. Arrange the patties on a baking sheet lined with parchment paper and sprinkle with olive oil.

6. Put the dish in the oven and bake it for 20 minutes.

7. Serve hot with tahini sauce or other desired condiments.

13. Veggie Quesadillas - Preparation time: 15 minutes

Ingredients:

- 4 small whole wheat tortillas

- 1/2 cup cooked vegetables of your choice (such as broccoli, carrots, bell pepper, mushrooms, etc.)

- 1/4 cup cooked beans of your choice (such as black beans, chickpeas, etc.)

- 1/4 cup vegan cheese, shredded

- 2 tablespoons freshly chopped cilantro

- 2 tablespoons olive oil

Instructions:

1. In a big skillet over medium heat, warm the olive oil.

2. Add one tortilla to the griddle and top with the beans, cheese, cilantro, and vegetables.

3. Add a second tortilla on top, then cook for two minutes.

4. After 2 minutes, flip the quesadilla over.

5. Carry out step five with the remaining tortillas.

6. Serve the quesadillas with salsa or other condiments of your choice after cutting them into wedges.

14. Lentil and Kale Salad, 25 minutes to prepare

Ingredients:

- 1 cup rinsed and drained dried lentils

- 2 cups vegetable broth

- 2 tablespoons olive oil

- 1 onion, diced

- 2 cloves garlic, minced

- 1/2 teaspoon sea salt

- 1/4 teaspoon freshly ground black pepper

- 4 cups kale, stemmed and chopped

- 2 tablespoons freshly squeezed lemon juice

Instructions:

1. Place the lentils and vegetable broth in a large pot and bring to a simmer.

2. Simmer for 20 minutes, stirring occasionally.

3. In a big skillet over medium heat, warm the olive oil.

4. Add the onion and garlic and simmer for 4 minutes or until tender.

5. Cook for 1 minute after adding the salt and pepper.

Kale is added and cooked for 5 minutes.

7. Include the cooked lentils and mix by stirring.

8. Turn the heat off and add the lemon juice.

9. Present warm or cold.

15. Baked Sweet Potato Fries - 25 minutes to prepare

Ingredients: - 2 big, peeled, and sliced sweet potatoes

- 2 tablespoons olive oil

- 1 teaspoon sea salt

- 1/2 teaspoon freshly ground black pepper

- 2 tablespoons freshly chopped parsley

Instructions:

1. Preheat the oven to 400°F (200°C).

2. Place the sweet potato wedges on a parchment-lined baking sheet and drizzle with olive oil.

3. Sprinkle with salt and pepper.

4. Bake in the preheated oven for 20 minutes, flipping once halfway through.

5. Sprinkle with the parsley and serve.

16. Coconut Quinoa Porridge - Preparation time: 25 minutes

Ingredients:

- 1 cup quinoa, rinsed and drained

- 2 cups coconut milk

- 2 tablespoons freshly chopped cilantro

- 2 tablespoons freshly chopped mint

- 2 tablespoons freshly chopped basil

- 1/2 teaspoon ground cinnamon

- 1/4 teaspoon freshly ground nutmeg

- 1/4 teaspoon sea salt

- 2 tablespoons shredded coconut

Instructions:

1. Place the quinoa and coconut milk in a medium pot and bring to a simmer.

2. Simmer for 20 minutes, stirring occasionally.

3. Remove from the heat and stir in the cilantro, mint, basil, cinnamon, nutmeg, and salt.

4. Divide the porridge among four bowls and top with the shredded coconut.

5. Serve warm.

17. Baked Avocado Fries - Preparation time: 25 minutes

Ingredients:

- two ripe avocados, peeled, and sliced into wedges.

- A serving of breadcrumbs

- 1/4 teaspoon dried garlic

- 1/4 teaspoon of onion powder

- One-fourth teaspoon sea salt

- 2 tablespoons of olive oil

- 1/4 teaspoon freshly ground black pepper

Instructions:

1. Set the oven temperature to 375°F (190°C).

2. Put the avocado wedges in a bowl that is not too deep.

3. Combine the breadcrumbs, garlic powder, onion powder, salt, and pepper in a different shallow bowl.

4. Coat each avocado wedge by dipping it in the breadcrumb mixture.

5. Arrange the olive oil-coated avocado wedges on a baking sheet lined with parchment paper.

6. Bake for 20 minutes in the preheated oven.

7. Present warm with your preferred dipping sauce.

18. Roasted Brussels Sprouts - Preparation time: 25 minutes

Ingredients:

- 2 tablespoons olive oil

- 2 cloves garlic, minced

- 1/2 teaspoon sea salt

- 1/4 teaspoon freshly ground black pepper

- 1 pound of halved and trimmed Brussels sprouts

- 2 tablespoons freshly chopped parsley

Instructions:

1. Preheat the oven to 400°F (200°C).

2. Place the olive oil, garlic, salt, and pepper in a large bowl and whisk to combine.

3. Add the Brussels sprouts and toss to coat.

4. Place the Brussels sprouts on a parchment-lined baking sheet and roast in the preheated oven for 20 minutes.

5. Sprinkle with parsley and serve hot.

19. Zucchini Noodle Bowl - Preparation time: 20 minutes

Ingredients:

- 2 tablespoons sesame oil

- 1 onion, diced

- 2 cloves garlic, minced

- 1 teaspoon freshly grated ginger

- 1/2 teaspoon sea salt

- 1/4 teaspoon freshly ground black pepper

- 2 medium zucchinis, spiralized

- 1 cup cooked vegetables of your choice (such as broccoli, carrots, bell pepper, mushrooms, etc.)

- 1/2 cup cooked beans of your choice (such as black beans, chickpeas, etc.)

- 2 tablespoons tamari

- 2 tablespoons freshly chopped cilantro

Instructions:

1. Heat the sesame oil in a large skillet over medium heat.

2. Add the onion and garlic and cook until softened, about 4 minutes.

3. Add the ginger, salt, and pepper and cook for 1 minute.

4. Add the zucchini noodles and cook for 5 minutes.

5. Add the cooked vegetables and beans and cook for 5 more minutes.

6. Stir in the tamari and cilantro and season with additional salt and pepper to taste.

7. Serve hot.

20. Eggplant Lasagna - Preparation time: 45 minutes

Ingredients:

- 2 tablespoons olive oil

- 1 onion, diced

- 2 cloves garlic, minced

- 1 can (14.5 oz) diced tomatoes

- 1/2 teaspoon sea salt

- 1/4 teaspoon freshly ground black pepper

- 1 large eggplant, sliced into 1/4-inch thick rounds

- 1/2 cup vegan ricotta cheese

- 1/2 cup vegan mozzarella cheese, shredded

- 2 tablespoons freshly chopped basil

Instructions:

1. Preheat the oven to 375°F (190°C).

2. In a big skillet over medium heat, warm the olive oil.

3. Add the onion and garlic and cook until softened, about 4 minutes.

4. Add the tomatoes, salt, and pepper and simmer for 10 minutes.

5. Place half of the eggplant slices in the bottom of a 9-inch baking dish.

6. Top with half of the tomato sauce, followed by half of the ricotta and mozzarella cheese.

7. Top with the remaining eggplant slices and tomato sauce.

8. Sprinkle with the remaining ricotta and mozzarella cheese.

9. Bake in the preheated oven for 25 minutes.

10. Sprinkle with the basil and serve hot.

52

CHAPTER FIVE

Recipes For Dinner

1. Quinoa and Chickpea Salad Components: 1 cup cooked quinoa, 1 can chickpeas, 1 bell pepper diced, 1/2 red onion, 2 tablespoons olive oil, 1 teaspoon cumin, 1 lemon's juice, Salt and pepper to taste.

Instructions: Quinoa, chickpeas, bell pepper, and red onion should all be combined in a big bowl. Mix the olive oil, lemon juice, and cumin in a small bowl. Toss the quinoa and vegetables together after adding the dressing. To taste, add salt and pepper to the food.

Time Spent Preparing: 10 minutes.

2. Creamy Pumpkin Soup: Ingredients: 6 cups vegetable broth, 2 cups canned pumpkin puree, 1/4 cup coconut milk, Salt and pepper to taste, 2 tablespoons olive oil, 1 onion, 2 cloves garlic, 2 tablespoons fresh ginger, 2 teaspoons ground cumin, and 2 teaspoons ground coriander.

Instructions: Over medium heat, warm the olive oil in a big pot. Cook the onion and garlic for about 5 minutes, or until tender. Cook the ginger, cumin, and coriander for one minute after adding them. Bring to a boil after adding the pumpkin puree and vegetable broth. After lowering the heat, let the food simmer for ten minutes. Add the coconut milk after seasoning to taste with salt and pepper.

Duration of preparation: 15 minutes.

3. Lentil Burgers: 1 cup cooked lentils, 1/4 cup rolled oats, 1/4 cup breadcrumbs, 1/4 cup shredded carrot, 1/4 cup diced onion, 1 clove of garlic, 1 tablespoon of extra virgin olive oil, 1 teaspoon of crushed cumin, 1 teaspoon of smoky paprika, and salt and pepper to taste.

Instructions: Lentils, oats, breadcrumbs, carrots, onions, and garlic should all be combined in a sizable basin. Mix the cumin, smoked paprika, and olive oil in a small bowl. After adding the lentils, stir the mixture thoroughly. Season the mixture with salt and pepper after forming it into 4 patties. The patties are added to a hot, big skillet over medium heat. Cook until golden brown, about 5 minutes per side.

Duration of preparation: 15 minutes.

4. Stir-fried vegetables:

Ingredients: 1 cup sliced mushrooms, 1 cup broccoli florets, 1 cup snow peas, 2 tablespoons soy sauce, 1 teaspoon sesame oil, 2 tablespoons vegetable oil, 2 garlic cloves, 1 onion, 1 red bell pepper.

Instructions: Over medium heat, warm the vegetable oil in a big skillet. Cook the garlic and onion for about 5 minutes, or until they are tender. Cook for 5 minutes after adding the bell pepper, broccoli, snow peas, and mushrooms. One minute later, add the soy sauce and sesame oil. Serve with cooked quinoa or rice.

Time Spent Preparing: 10 minutes.

5. Sweet Potato and Kale Curry: 2 tablespoons vegetable oil, 1 onion, 2 garlic cloves, 1 tablespoon freshly grated ginger, 2 teaspoons each of ground cumin, coriander, turmeric, and garam masala, 2 cups of vegetable broth, 1 can of coconut milk, 2 sweet potatoes, and 2 cups of chopped kale. To taste, add salt and pepper.

Instructions: Over medium heat, warm the vegetable oil in a big pot. Cook the onion and garlic for about 5 minutes, or until tender. Cook for one minute after adding the ginger, cumin, coriander, turmeric, and garam masala. Bring to a boil the sweet potatoes, coconut milk, and vegetable broth. After lowering the heat, let the food simmer for ten minutes. After adding, simmer the greens for 5 minutes. To taste, add salt and pepper to the food. Serve with cooked quinoa or rice.

Duration of preparation: 15 minutes.

6. Vegetable-Stuffed Peppers: This recipe calls for 2 tablespoons of olive oil, 1 onion, 2 cloves of garlic, 1 cup of cooked quinoa, 1

can of black beans, 1/2 cup of corn, 1 teaspoon of cumin, 1 teaspoon of smoked paprika, 4 bell peppers, and 1/2 cup of shredded vegan cheese. Salt and pepper are also added to taste.

Instructions: Set the oven to 400 °F. Over medium heat, warm the olive oil in a large skillet. Cook the onion and garlic for about 5 minutes, or until tender. Cook for 5 minutes after adding the quinoa, black beans, corn, cumin, and smoked paprika. Bell peppers should be seeded and cut in half. The quinoa mixture should be placed inside of each pepper, followed by the vegan cheese. In a baking dish, arrange the stuffed peppers, and bake for 15 minutes, or until the peppers are soft. To taste, add salt and pepper to the food.

Time Spent Preparing: 20 minutes.

7. Roasted Eggplant and Tomato Stew: 2 tablespoons of extra virgin olive oil, 1 onion, 2 cloves of garlic, 2 eggplants, 2 cans of diced tomatoes, 1 teaspoon each of dried oregano and basil, 1 teaspoon each of smoked paprika, and salt and pepper to taste.

Instructions: Set the oven to 400 °F. Over medium heat, warm the olive oil in a large skillet. Cook the onion and garlic for about 5 minutes, or until tender. Add the 1-inch cubes of cubed eggplant to the skillet. For five minutes, cook. Cook for 10 minutes after adding the tomatoes, oregano, basil, and smoked paprika. When the eggplant is cooked, transfer the mixture to a baking dish and bake for 20 minutes. To taste, add salt and pepper to the food.

Duration of preparation: 25 minutes.

8. Quinoa Pilaf: This dish contains the following ingredients: 2 teaspoons of extra virgin olive oil, 1 onion, 2 cloves of garlic, 1 cup of quinoa, 2 cups of vegetable broth, 1/2 cup of chopped almonds, 1/2 cup of dried cranberries, and salt and pepper to taste.

Instructions: Over medium heat, warm the olive oil in a large skillet. Cook the onion and garlic for about 5 minutes, or until tender. Quinoa is then added and cooked for 2 minutes. Bring it to a boil after including the veggie broth. Once the quinoa is cooked, reduce the heat to low and let it simmer for 15 minutes. Add the cranberries and almonds after seasoning to taste with salt and pepper.

Duration of preparation: 15 minutes.

9. Stuffed Sweet Potatoes: 4 sweet potatoes, 2 tablespoons olive oil, 1 onion, 2 garlic cloves, 1 can of black beans, 1/2 cup of corn, 1 teaspoon cumin, 1 teaspoon smoky paprika, and 1/2 cup of shredded vegan cheese. Salt and pepper to taste.

Instructions: Set the oven to 400 °F. Bake the sweet potatoes for 30 minutes, or until they are cooked, after poking them with a fork. Over medium heat, warm the olive oil in a large skillet. Cook the onion and garlic for about 5 minutes, or until tender. Cook for 5 minutes after adding the black beans, corn, cumin, and smoked paprika. Scoop out the flesh after cutting the sweet potatoes in half. The sweet potato flesh should be mashed and added to the skillet. Mix thoroughly, then add salt and pepper to taste. The mixture is placed into the sweet potatoes, then the vegan cheese is added on top. To melt the cheese, bake the dish for 10 minutes.

Time Spent Preparing: 40 minutes.

10. Spicy tofu: 1 package extra-firm tofu, 2 tablespoons soy sauce, 2 teaspoons sriracha, 2 teaspoons sesame oil, salt and pepper to taste, 2 tablespoons vegetable oil, 1 onion, 2 cloves of garlic, and 2 tablespoons sesame oil.

Instructions: Over medium heat, warm the vegetable oil in a big skillet. Cook the onion and garlic for about 5 minutes, or until tender. While cooking the tofu for 5 minutes, stir it occasionally. Cook for one minute after adding the sesame oil, soy sauce, and sriracha. To taste, add salt and pepper to the food.

Time Spent Preparing: 10 minutes.

11. Baked Tempeh and Vegetables: This dish is made with 2 tablespoons of olive oil, 1 onion, 2 cloves of garlic, 1 package of tempeh, 2 cups of sliced mushrooms, 1 red bell pepper, 1/2 cup of frozen corn, 2 tablespoons of soy sauce, and 1 teaspoon of smoked paprika. Salt and pepper are added to taste.

Instructions: Set the oven to 400 °F. Over medium heat, warm the olive oil in a large skillet. Cook the onion and garlic for about 5 minutes, or until tender. Cook the tempeh for 5 minutes after adding it. Cook the corn, bell pepper, and mushrooms for 5 minutes more. For one minute, add the soy sauce and smoked paprika. When the veggies are soft, transfer the mixture to a baking dish and bake for 15 minutes. To taste, add salt and pepper to the food.

Time Spent Preparing: 20 minutes.

12. Roasted Vegetable Wrap: 4 whole wheat tortillas, 2 tablespoons soy sauce, 1/2 cup sliced mushrooms, 1 red bell pepper, 2 cloves of garlic, 1 zucchini, and salt and pepper to taste.

Instructions: Set the oven to 400 °F. Over medium heat, warm the olive oil in a large skillet. Cook the onion and garlic for about 5 minutes, or until tender. Cook for 5 minutes after adding the bell pepper, zucchini, and mushrooms. Cook for one minute after adding the soy sauce. When the veggies are soft, transfer the mixture to a baking dish and bake for 15 minutes. Sprinkle the tortillas with salt and pepper, then top with the roasted vegetables.

Time Spent Preparing: 20 minutes.

13. Veggie quesadillas: 4 whole wheat tortillas, 1/2 cup shredded vegan cheese, salt and pepper to taste, 2 tablespoons olive oil, 1 onion, 2 cloves of garlic, 1 red bell pepper, 1 cup frozen corn.

Instructions: Over medium heat, warm the olive oil in a large skillet. Cook the onion and garlic for about 5 minutes, or until tender. Five minutes later, add the corn, bell pepper, and soy sauce. With the roasted vegetables and vegan cheese, place 2 tortillas in the griddle. The remaining tortillas should be placed on top, and the cheese should melt after 5 minutes of cooking. Toss the quesadillas with salt and pepper to taste after cutting them into wedges.

Duration of preparation: 15 minutes.

14. Eggplant Lasagna: 2 tablespoons of olive oil, 1 onion, 2 cloves of garlic, 2 eggplants, 2 cans of diced tomatoes, 2 teaspoons of tomato paste, 1 teaspoon each of dried oregano and smoky paprika, 2 cups of vegan ricotta cheese, 4 lasagna noodles, and salt and pepper to taste.

Instructions: Set the oven to 350°F. Over medium heat, warm the olive oil in a large skillet. Cook the onion and garlic for about 5 minutes, or until tender. Add the 1-inch cubes of cubed eggplant to the skillet. For five minutes, cook. Cook for 10 minutes after adding the tomatoes, tomato paste, oregano, and smoked paprika. The sauce should be layered at the bottom of a baking dish. Two lasagna noodles, half of the vegan ricotta, and a layer of sauce are placed on top. Layer again, then drizzle the remaining sauce on top. Bake the lasagna for 30 minutes, or until well heated. To taste, add salt and pepper to the food.

Time Spent Preparing: 40 minutes.

15. Baked Zucchini Fritters: This recipe calls for two zucchini, half a cup of bread crumbs, two teaspoons of vegan Parmesan cheese, two tablespoons of almond flour, one teaspoon of dried oregano, one teaspoon of garlic powder, two tablespoons of olive oil, and salt and pepper to taste.

Instructions: Set the oven to 400 °F. Zucchini should be grated and put in a big bowl. Combine the bread crumbs, almond flour, oregano, garlic powder, vegan Parmesan cheese, and olive oil. Put the mixture on a baking sheet and shape it into tiny patties. Once golden brown, bake for another 15 minutes. To taste, add salt and pepper to the food.

Time Spent Preparing: 10 minutes

16. Veggie Burrito Bowl: 2 tablespoons of olive oil, 1 onion, 2 garlic cloves, 1 red bell pepper, 1 zucchini, 1/2 cup of sliced mushrooms, 2 tablespoons of soy sauce, 2 cups of cooked brown rice, 1 can of black beans, 1/2 cup of corn, and salt and pepper to taste.

Instructions: Over medium heat, warm the olive oil in a large skillet. Cook the onion and garlic for about 5 minutes, or until tender. Cook for 5 minutes after adding the bell pepper, zucchini, and mushrooms. Cook for one minute after adding the soy sauce. Add the roasted vegetables to a bowl of brown rice, black beans, and corn. To taste, add salt and pepper to the food.

Duration of preparation: 15 minutes.

17. Spinach and Chickpea Coconut Curry: 2 tablespoons of vegetable oil, 1 onion, 2 cloves of garlic, 2 teaspoons of freshly grated ginger, 2 teaspoons of crushed cumin, 2 teaspoons of ground coriander, 2 teaspoons of turmeric, 1 can of coconut milk, 1 can of chickpeas, and 2 cups of spinach. To taste, add salt and pepper.

Instructions: Over medium heat, warm the vegetable oil in a big pot. Cook the onion and garlic for about 5 minutes, or until tender. Cook for one minute after adding the ginger, cumin, coriander, and turmeric. Bring the chickpeas and coconut milk to a boil before adding the latter. After lowering the heat, let the food simmer for ten minutes. Cook the spinach for 5 minutes after adding it. To taste, add salt and pepper to the food. Serve with cooked quinoa or rice.

Duration of preparation: 15 minutes.

18. Avocado Toast: This dish consists of two pieces of whole wheat bread, one avocado, two tablespoons of extra virgin olive oil, one lemon's juice, one teaspoon of smoked paprika, and salt and pepper to taste.

Instructions: The bread slices are toast. Mash the avocado with the lemon juice, smoked paprika, and olive oil in a small bowl. Add salt and pepper to taste before spreading the avocado mixture on the toast.

5 minutes are needed for preparation.

19. Vegetable Fried Rice: 2 tablespoons of vegetable oil, 1 onion, 2 garlic cloves, 2 cups of cooked brown rice, 1 cup of frozen mixed vegetables, 2 tablespoons of soy sauce, 2 teaspoons of sesame oil, and salt and pepper to taste.

Instructions: Over medium heat, warm the vegetable oil in a big skillet. Cook the onion and garlic for about 5 minutes, or until tender. Cook for 5 minutes after adding the brown rice and frozen veggies. One minute later, add the soy sauce and sesame oil. To taste, add salt and pepper to the food.

Time Spent Preparing: 10 minutes.

20. Roasted Cauliflower Salad: 1 head of cauliflower, 2 teaspoons of extra-virgin olive oil, 1/2 cup of sliced almonds, 1/2 cup of dried cranberries, 1/2 cup of vegan feta cheese, juice from 1 lemon, 2 tablespoons of freshly chopped parsley, and salt and pepper to taste.

Instructions: Set the oven to 400 °F. The cauliflower should be divided into florets and put on a baking sheet. Sprinkle with salt and pepper and drizzle with olive oil. Roast until soft, about 15 minutes. Put the roasted cauliflower, almonds, cranberries, vegan feta cheese, lemon juice, and parsley in a large bowl. Add salt and pepper to taste and toss to mix.

Time Spent Preparing: 20 minutes.

CHAPTER SIX

Snack Recipes

Banana-walnut muffins,

turn the oven on to 350 degrees. 2 mashed bananas, 1 cup of flour, 1/2 cup of sugar, 1/4 cup of vegetable oil, 1 teaspoon baking soda, 1/2 teaspoon salt, and 1/2 cup of walnuts should all be combined in a medium basin. Just combine everything after combining. Each cup in a muffin tin should be filled with 1/4 cup of the batter. For 20 minutes, bake.

2. Fried zucchini

2 cups of grated zucchini, 1/2 cup of flour, 1/4 cup of nutritional yeast, 3 tablespoons of olive oil, 1 teaspoon each of garlic powder, onion powder, baking powder, and baking soda, along with a dash of salt, should all be combined in a food processor. Until the mixture is well-combined, pulse together. 1 tablespoon of olive oil has been added to a big skillet that's been heated up over medium heat. Create small patties from the zucchini mixture, and fry them in the skillet for 4-5 minutes on each side, or until golden brown.

3. Toasted Avocado

1 piece of toast with 1/2 an avocado smeared on it. Add 1/4 cup of diced red onion, 1/4 cup of cherry tomatoes, and a dash of sea salt to finish.

4. Sweet potato chips,

A 400 degree oven is recommended. 1 sweet potato should be thinly sliced. Place the slices on a baking sheet that has been prepared, and then brush with the olive oil. Add some black pepper and sea salt. Bake the chips for 15-20 minutes, or until crisp and golden brown.

5. Veggies and hummus

1 can of chickpeas, 2 tablespoons of tahini, 1 teaspoon each of cumin, garlic powder, and sea salt, along with 1/4 cup of water, should be combined in a medium bowl. Until smooth, blend. Serve with dipping vegetables like carrots, celery, and bell peppers.

6. Fruit Salad

2 cups of chopped pineapple, 2 cups of diced mango, 2 cups of diced papaya, 1 cup of diced strawberries, and 1/4 cup of shredded coconut should all be combined in a big dish. Mix everything together, then chill for at least one hour before serving.

7. Trail Mix

1 cup of rolled oats, 1/2 cup of chopped walnuts, 1/2 cup of dried cranberries, 1/4 cup of dark chocolate chips, 1/4 cup of sunflower seeds, and 1/4 cup of pumpkin seeds should all be combined in a big bowl. Use an airtight container for storage.

8. Rubbed Chickpeas

A 400 degree oven is recommended. 1 can of chickpeas, 1 tablespoon of olive oil, and 1/2 teaspoon of garlic powder should all be combined in a medium bowl. Combine by tossing. On a greased baking sheet, spread the chickpeas evenly, and bake for 20 minutes, or until crispy.

9. Vegetable wraps

Each of the 2 tortillas should have 1/4 cup of hummus on it. Add a half cup of chopped lettuce, a quarter cup of diced tomatoes, a fourth cup of shredded carrots, and a fourth cup of diced cucumbers as a garnish. Roll out and have fun.

10. Sweet Potato Fries Fried in the Air

1 sweet potato should be thinly sliced. In an oiled air fryer basket, arrange the strips in a single layer. Air fried at 400 degrees for 10 minutes, or until golden and crispy.

11. Toast with almond butter

One slice of toast with one spoonful of almond butter on it. Sprinkle 1/4 cup of strawberry dice on top.

12. roasted vegetables

A 400 degree oven is recommended. 1/2 cup chopped carrots, 1/2 cup diced potatoes, 1/2 cup diced bell peppers, 1/4 cup diced red onion, 2 tablespoons olive oil, and 1/4 teaspoon sea salt should all be combined in a big bowl. Combine by tossing. On a prepared baking sheet, spread the vegetables evenly, and bake for 20 minutes, or until they are soft.

13. Apple slices with peanut butter

Cut one apple into small wedges. One spoonful of peanut butter should be spread on each slice.

14. Edamame

Bring 1/2 cup of edamame and 1/2 cup of water to a boil in a medium pot. Cook the edamame for 5 minutes or until it is soft after reducing the heat to a simmer. Add 1/4 teaspoon of sea salt after draining.

15. Lentil Soup

2 tablespoons of olive oil are heated over medium heat in a big pot. 1/2 cup of diced onion should be added and cooked until soft. 6 cups of vegetable broth, 1 teaspoon of garlic powder, and 1 cup of dried lentils should be added. Simmer after bringing to a boil. Cook the lentils for 25 minutes, or until they are soft.

16. Guacamole

In a medium bowl, combine 2 mashed avocados, 1/4 cup of diced red onion, 1/4 cup of diced tomatoes, 1/4 cup of cilantro, 1/2 teaspoon of garlic powder, and 1/4 teaspoon of sea salt. Mix together until combined.

17. Energy Bites

In a medium bowl, combine 1/2 cup of rolled oats, 1/2 cup of almond butter, 1/4 cup of maple syrup, 1/4 cup of ground flaxseed, 1/4 cup of mini chocolate chips, and 1/4 teaspoon of ground cinnamon. Mix together until combined. Form the mixture into 1-inch balls and refrigerate for 1 hour before serving.

18. Fruit Smoothie

In a blender, combine 1 cup of frozen mango chunks, 1/2 banana, 1/2 cup of orange juice, and 1/2 cup of plain non-dairy yogurt. Blend until smooth.

19. Baked Apples

Preheat oven to 375 degrees. Core 2 apples and place in a greased baking dish. In a small bowl, combine 3 tablespoons of brown sugar, 1/2 teaspoon of ground cinnamon, and 1 tablespoon of melted coconut oil. Mix together until combined. Spoon the mixture into the apples and bake for 20 minutes or until the apples are tender.

20. Popcorn

In a small saucepan, heat 1 tablespoon of coconut oil over medium heat. Cover after including 1/2 cup of popcorn kernels. Shake the pan every few minutes until the kernels have stopped popping. Remove from heat and season with sea salt and black pepper. Enjoy.

CHAPTER SEVEN

Dessert Recipes

1. Apple Crumble with Caramel

Set the oven to 350°F. 4 medium apples should be peeled, cored, and sliced thin before being placed in a greased 9x13 inch baking dish. Combine 1/4 cup brown sugar, 1/4 cup all-purpose flour, 1/4 tsp ground cinnamon, and 2 tablespoons vegan margarine in a medium bowl. The apples should be covered with the crumble mixture. Bake for 30 minutes, or until golden brown, in a preheated oven. With vegan ice cream, serve warm. Time Required: 15 minutes for preparation; 30 minutes for cooking.

2. Cookie Dough Bites with Chocolate Chips

Combine 1/2 cup vegan margarine, 1/2 cup coconut sugar, 1/2 teaspoon vanilla extract, and 1/4 teaspoon almond extract in a medium bowl. Add 2 cups of all-purpose flour gradually, then incorporate 1/2 cup of vegan semi-sweet chocolate chips. Create little balls out of the dough and set them on a baking sheet that has been buttered. Bake for 12 minutes @ 350°F or until golden brown in a preheated oven. 10 minutes are spent on preparation; 12 minutes are spent cooking.

3. Chocolate Chip Muffins with Bananas

Mix 1-1/2 cups all-purpose flour, 1/4 cup coconut sugar, 1 tsp baking powder, and 1/2 tsp baking soda in a medium bowl. 1 mashed banana, 1/4 cup vegan margarine, 1/4 cup non-dairy milk, and 1 teaspoon vanilla extract should all be combined in a different bowl. Add the dry ingredients gradually, then stir in half a cup of vegan semi-sweet chocolate chips. Pour the batter into a prepared muffin tin and bake at 350°F for 15-20 minutes, or until a toothpick inserted in the center comes out clean. Time Required: 10 minutes for preparation; 15 to 20 minutes for cooking.

4. Tofu Pie

Set the oven to 375°F. Butter a 9-inch pie plate. 1 package of silken tofu, 1/4 cup non-dairy milk, 1/4 cup vegan margarine, 1/4 cup coconut sugar, and 1 teaspoon vanilla extract should all be combined in a medium bowl. Place the pie dish with the mixture inside, and bake for 25 minutes. Before serving, allow cooling. Time Required: 10 minutes for preparation; 25 minutes for cooking.

5. Fudge with peanut butter

Mix 1/2 cup vegan margarine, 1/2 cup peanut butter, 1/2 cup coconut sugar, and 1/4 cup non-dairy milk in a medium pot. Cook the mixture until it boils while stirring continuously over medium heat. Pour into an 8x8-inch buttered baking dish after removing from the heat. Before cutting into squares, allow it cool. 10 minutes are spent on preparation; 10 minutes are spent cooking.

6. Fruit Salad

4 cups of diced fresh fruit, including apples, oranges, bananas, and berries, should be combined in a big bowl. Add 1/4 cup of lemon juice and 1/4 cup of coconut sugar. Stir gently to blend. Before serving, place in the fridge for at least one hour. Time Required: 15 minutes for preparation; 1 hour for cooking.

7. Avocado Chocolate Pudding

1 ripe avocado, 1/4 cup cocoa powder, 1/4 cup coconut sugar, 1/4 cup non-dairy milk, and 1 teaspoon vanilla extract are all combined in a food processor. Until smooth, blend. Before serving, place in the fridge for at least one hour. Time Required: 10 minutes for preparation; 1 hour for cooking.

8. Granola bars with chocolate and coconut

Set the oven to 350°F. Combine 1/2 cup of rolled oats, 1/4 cup of coconut flakes, 1/4 cup of vegan semi-sweet chocolate chips, and 1/4 cup of chopped almonds in a medium bowl. Mix 1/4 cup vegan margarine, 1/4 cup maple syrup, and 1/2 tsp vanilla extract in a another bowl. Add the dry ingredients gradually and blend thereafter. In a greased 9x13-inch baking dish, spread the mixture, and bake for 25 minutes, or until golden brown. Before cutting into bars, let cool. Time Required: 10 minutes for preparation; 25 minutes for cooking.

9. Macaroons with coconut

Set the oven to 350°F. Mix 1/2 cup coconut shreds, 1/4 cup all-purpose flour, 1/4 cup coconut sugar, and 1/4 cup vegan margarine in a medium bowl. Place the mixture's little balls on a baking sheet that has been buttered. 10 minutes in the oven, or until golden brown. 10 minutes are spent on preparation; 10 minutes are spent cooking.

10. Strawberry Coconut Creme Pancake

Combine 1 cup plain non-dairy yogurt, 2 tablespoons coconut sugar, and 1/2 teaspoon vanilla extract in a medium bowl. Combine 1/2 cup chopped strawberries, 1/4 cup shredded coconut, and 1/4 cup vegan semi-sweet chocolate chips in a another bowl. In a parfait glass, layer the strawberry mixture and yogurt mixture. Before serving, chill. 10 minutes for preparation; 0 minutes for cooking.

11. Cookies with dates

Set the oven to 350°F. 1 cup pitted dates, 1/4 cup coconut sugar, 1/4 cup vegan margarine, and 1/4 tsp ground cinnamon should all be combined in a food processor. Pulse the mixture until a paste forms. Drop the date mixture by tablespoons onto a baking sheet that has been buttered. 10 minutes in the oven, or until golden brown. 10 minutes are spent on preparation; 10 minutes are spent cooking.

12. Smoothie with apple crumble

1/4 cup plain non-dairy yogurt, 1/4 cup rolled oats, 1/4 cup vegan semi-sweet chocolate chips, and 1/4 tsp ground cinnamon are all combined in a blender with 1/2 cup chopped apples. Until smooth, blend. Add 1 tablespoon of chopped nuts and 1 tablespoon of coconut flakes to the glass after pouring. 5 minutes for preparation; 0 minutes for cooking.

13. Coconut Ice Cream That Is Vegan

1 can of full-fat coconut milk, 1/4 cup coconut sugar, and 1/2 teaspoon vanilla extract should all be combined in a medium bowl. Assemble by combining. Fill an ice cream machine with the mixture, then freeze it as directed by the manufacturer. Offer cold. 5 minutes for preparation; cooking times vary depending on the ice cream maker.

14. Baked Apples

Set the oven to 350°F. A 9x13-inch baking pan should be greased. 4 medium apples, cored, should be placed in the dish. Mix 1/4 cup raisins, 1/4 cup vegan margarine, 1/4 cup coconut sugar, 1/4 tsp cinnamon, and 1/4 tsp nutmeg in a medium bowl. Place the mixture inside the apples and bake for 25 minutes, or until the apples are soft, in a preheated oven. Serve hot. Time Required: 10 minutes for preparation; 25 minutes for cooking.

15. Chocolate Peanut Butter No-Bake Bars

Mix 1/2 cup vegan margarine, 1/2 cup peanut butter, 1/4 cup cocoa powder, 1/4 cup coconut sugar, and 1/4 cup non-dairy milk together in a medium bowl. Before cutting into bars, spread the mixture into an 8x8 inch oiled baking dish. Then, chill the dish for at least an hour. Time Required: 10 minutes for preparation; 1 hour for cooking.

16. Oatmeal Raisin Cookies

Set the oven to 350°F. Mix 1/2 cup vegan margarine, 1/2 cup coconut sugar, 1/2 cup all-purpose flour, 1/2 cup rolled oats, 1/4 teaspoon ground nutmeg, and 1/2 teaspoon ground cinnamon in a medium bowl. 1/4 cup of raisins are included. Drop spoonfuls of the mixture onto a baking sheet that has been buttered. 10 minutes in the oven, or until golden brown. 10 minutes are spent on preparation; 10 minutes are spent cooking.

17. Smoothie bowl with apple pie

1/2 cup chopped apples, 1/4 cup non-dairy milk, 1/4 cup plain non-dairy yogurt, and 1/4 tsp ground cinnamon should all be blended together. Until smooth, blend. Add 1 tbsp of chopped walnuts, 1 tbsp of shredded coconut, and 1 tbsp of vegan semi-sweet chocolate chips on top of the mixture once you've poured it into a bowl. 5 minutes for preparation; 0 minutes for cooking.

18. Banana Walnut Bread

Set the oven to 350°F. Butter a 9x5-inch loaf pan. 1-1/2 cups all-purpose flour, 1/4 cup coconut sugar, 1 tsp baking powder, and 1/2 tsp baking soda should be combined in a medium bowl. 1 mashed banana, 1/4 cup vegan margarine, 1/4 cup non-dairy milk, and 1/2 tsp vanilla extract should all be combined in a different bowl. Fold in half a cup of the chopped walnuts after adding the dry ingredients gradually. Fill the pan with the mixture, and bake it for 40 minutes, or until a toothpick inserted into the center comes out clean. Time Required: 10 minutes for preparation; 40 minutes for cooking.

19. Fudge with chocolate and peanut butter

Mix 1/2 cup peanut butter, 1/2 cup vegan margarine, 1/2 cup coconut sugar, and 1/4 cup non-dairy milk in a medium pot. Cook the mixture until it boils while stirring continuously over medium heat. Add 1/4 cup of cocoa powder after taking the pan from the heat. In an 8x8-inch baking dish that has been buttered, pour the mixture. Before cutting into squares, allow it cool. 10 minutes are spent on preparation; 10 minutes are spent cooking.

20. Popcorn with coconut caramel

1/4 cup vegan margarine, 1/4 cup coconut sugar, and 1/4 cup non-dairy milk should all be combined in a medium saucepan. Cook the mixture until it boils while stirring continuously over medium heat. After removing from the heat, toss in 1/4 cup of coconut shreds. Mix the contents of the recipe thoroughly before adding 6 cups of popcorn. The mixture should be spread out onto a baking sheet that has been oiled and baked for 10 minutes at 350°F or until golden brown. 10 minutes are spent on preparation; 10 minutes are spent cooking.

CHAPTER EIGHT

Beverage Recipes

1. Beetroot Juice - Preparation Time: 10 minutes

Ingredients:

-2 large beetroots

-2 carrots

-1/2 a cucumber

-1/2 an apple

-1/4 lemon

Instructions:

1. Peel and cut the beetroots into cubes.

2. Peel and cut the carrots into cubes.

3. Peel and chop the cucumber.

4. Peel and core the apple and cut it into cubes.

5. Place all the vegetables into a blender and blend until smooth.

6. Squeeze in the lemon juice and blend again.

7. Strain through a sieve and serve.

2. Green Smoothie - Preparation Time: 10 minutes

Ingredients:

-1 cup of spinach

-1 banana

-1/2 an apple

-1/2 cup of almond milk

-1 teaspoon of honey

Instructions:

1. Place the spinach, banana, and apple into a blender and blend until smooth.

2. Add the almond milk and honey and blend again.

3. Strain through a sieve and serve.

3. Coconut Water - Preparation Time: 5 minutes

Ingredients:

-1 cup of coconut water

-1/2 cup of pineapple juice

-1/4 cup of lime juice

Instructions:

1. Place the coconut water, pineapple juice, and lime juice into a blender and blend until smooth.

2. Strain through a sieve and serve.

4. Tomato Juice - Preparation Time: 10 minutes

Ingredients:

-2 tomatoes

-1/2 a cucumber

-1/2 an onion

-1/4 cup of parsley

-1/4 cup of celery

-1 teaspoon of black pepper

Instructions:

1. Peel and chop the tomatoes.

2. Peel and chop the cucumber.

3. Peel and chop the onion.

4. Place all the vegetables into a blender and blend until smooth.

5. Strain through a sieve and add the parsley, celery, and black pepper.

6. Stir to combine and serve.

5. Mint Lemonade - Preparation Time: 10 minutes

Ingredients:

-1/2 cup of mint leaves

-2 cups of water

-1/2 cup of honey

-1/2 cup of lemon juice

Instructions:

1. Place the mint leaves and water into a saucepan and bring to a boil.

2. Reduce the heat and let the mixture simmer for 5 minutes.

3. Strain and discard the leaves.

4. Add the honey and lemon juice and stir to combine.

5. Let the mixture cool and serve.

6. Carrot Juice - Preparation Time: 10 minutes

Ingredients:

-2 large carrots

-1/2 an apple

-1/4 cup of spinach

-1/4 cup of parsley

-1 teaspoon of ground ginger

Instructions:

1. Peel and cut the carrots into cubes.

2. Peel and core the apple and cut it into cubes.

3. Place all the ingredients into a blender and blend until smooth.

4. Strain through a sieve and serve.

7. Peach Iced Tea - Preparation Time: 10 minutes

Ingredients:

-2 peaches

-4 cups of water

-1/4 cup of honey

-1/4 cup of lemon juice

-2 teaspoons of tea leaves

Instructions:

1. Peel and chop the peaches into small pieces.

2. Place the water and peaches into a saucepan and bring to a boil.

3. Reduce the heat and let the mixture simmer for 5 minutes.

4. Strain and discard the peaches.

5. Add the honey, lemon juice, and tea leaves and stir to combine.

6. Let the mixture cool and serve.

8. Mango Lassi - Preparation Time: 10 minutes

Ingredients:

-1 mango

-1/2 cup of plain yogurt

-1/4 cup of honey

-1/4 cup of water

Instructions:

1. Peel and chop the mango into small pieces.

2. Place the mango, yogurt, honey, and water into a blender and blend until smooth.

3. Strain through a sieve and serve.

9. Watermelon Juice - Preparation Time: 10 minutes

Ingredients:

-2 cups of watermelon

-1/2 cup of orange juice

-1/4 cup of lemon juice

-1/4 cup of mint leaves

Instructions:

1. Cut the watermelon into cubes.

2. Place the watermelon, orange juice, lemon juice, and mint leaves into a blender and blend until smooth.

3. Strain through a sieve and serve.

10. Banana Milkshake - Preparation Time: 10 minutes

Ingredients:

-2 bananas

-1/2 cup of almond milk

-1/4 cup of honey

-1/4 teaspoon of ground cinnamon

Instructions:

1. Peel and cut the bananas into slices.

2. Place the bananas, almond milk, honey, and cinnamon into a blender and blend until smooth.

3. Strain through a sieve and serve.

11. Cranberry Juice - Preparation Time: 10 minutes

Ingredients:

-1 cup of cranberries

-1/2 cup of water

-1/4 cup of honey

-1/4 cup of lime juice

Instructions:

1. Place the cranberries and water into a saucepan and bring to a boil.

2. Reduce the heat and let the mixture simmer for 5 minutes.

3. Strain and discard the cranberries.

4. Add the honey and lime juice and stir to combine.

5. Let the mixture cool and serve.

12. Almond Milk Latte - Preparation Time: 10 minutes

Ingredients:

-1 cup of almond milk

-1/2 teaspoon of ground cinnamon

-1/4 teaspoon of ground nutmeg

-1/4 teaspoon of ground cardamom

Instructions:

1. Place the almond milk into a saucepan and bring to a simmer.

2. Remove from the heat and add the cinnamon, nutmeg, and cardamom.

3. Whisk to combine and let the mixture cool.

4. Serve in a mug.

13. Cucumber Mint Cooler - Preparation Time: 10 minutes

Ingredients:

-1 cucumber

-1/2 cup of mint leaves

-1/4 cup of honey

-1/4 cup of lime juice

Instructions:

1. Peel and chop the cucumber into small pieces.

2. Place the cucumber, mint leaves, honey, and lime juice into a blender and blend until smooth.

3. Strain through a sieve and serve.

14. Apple Juice - Preparation Time: 10 minutes

Ingredients:

-2 apples

-1/2 cup of water

-1/4 cup of honey

-1/4 cup of lemon juice

Instructions:

1. Peel and core the apples and cut them into cubes.

2. Place the apples and water into a saucepan and bring to a boil.

3. Reduce the heat and let the mixture simmer for 5 minutes.

4. Strain and discard the apples.

5. Add the honey and lemon juice and stir to combine.

6. Let the mixture cool and serve.

15. Turmeric Latte - Preparation Time: 10 minutes

Ingredients:

-1 cup of almond milk

-1 teaspoon of turmeric

-1/4 teaspoon of ground ginger

-1/4 teaspoon of ground cinnamon

Instructions:

1. Place the almond milk into a saucepan and bring to a simmer.

2. Remove from the heat and add the turmeric, ginger, and cinnamon.

3. Whisk to combine and let the mixture cool.

4. Serve in a mug.

16. Lemonade - Preparation Time: 10 minutes

Ingredients:

-1/2 cup of lemon juice

-1/4 cup of honey

-4 cups of water

Instructions:

1. Place the lemon juice, honey, and water into a blender and blend until combined.

2. Let the mixture cool and serve.

17. Strawberry Smoothie - Preparation Time: 10 minutes

Ingredients:

-2 cups of strawberries

-1 banana

-1/2 cup of almond milk

-1/4 cup of honey

Instructions:

1. Place the strawberries, banana, and almond milk into a blender and blend until smooth.

2. Add the honey and blend again.

3. Strain through a sieve and serve.

18. Ginger Tea - Preparation Time: 10 minutes

Ingredients:

-1 teaspoon of freshly grated ginger

-2 cups of water

-1/4 cup of honey

-1/4 cup of lemon juice

Instructions:

1. Place the ginger and water into a saucepan and bring to a boil.

2. Reduce the heat and let the mixture simmer for 5 minutes.

3. Strain and discard the ginger.

4. Add the honey and lemon juice and stir to combine.

5. Let the mixture cool and serve.

19. Pineapple Juice - Preparation Time: 10 minutes

Ingredients:

-2 cups of pineapple

-1/2 cup of water

-1/4 cup of honey

-1/4 cup of lime juice

Instructions:

1. Cut the pineapple into cubes.

2. Place the pineapple and water into a saucepan and bring to a boil.

3. Reduce the heat and let the mixture simmer for 5 minutes.

4. Strain and discard the pineapple.

5. Add the honey and lime juice and stir to combine.

6. Let the mixture cool and serve.

20. Green Tea - Preparation Time: 10 minutes

Ingredients:

-1 teaspoon of green tea leaves

-2 cups of water

-1/4 cup of honey

-1/4 cup of lemon juice

Instructions:

1. Place the tea leaves and water into a saucepan and bring to a boil.

2. Reduce the heat and let the mixture simmer for 5 minutes.

3. Strain and discard the tea leaves.

4. Add the honey and lemon juice and stir to combine.

5. Let the mixture cool and serve.

93

94

CHAPTER NINE

Nutritional Considerations For Cirrhosis

Nutritional considerations for cirrhosis are important because cirrhosis is a chronic liver condition that can lead to serious health complications. It is characterized by scarring of the liver and can be caused by a variety of factors such as chronic alcohol abuse, viral hepatitis, or other inherited diseases. Cirrhosis can lead to malnutrition, which can further worsen the condition. Adequate nutrition is essential for people with cirrhosis to maintain their overall health and minimize the risk of complications. A balanced diet is important for maintaining energy levels, keeping the body healthy, and providing the essential nutrients needed for maintaining normal liver function.

The most important nutritional consideration for people with cirrhosis is to maintain an adequate calorie intake. It is important to eat a balanced diet that includes adequate amounts of carbohydrates, proteins, and fats. Eating small, frequent meals may be beneficial for someone with cirrhosis as it can help them to better digest their food and absorb nutrients. Vitamins and minerals are also important for people with cirrhosis as they are essential for optimal health. Vitamin A, B-complex vitamins, and vitamin C can help to protect the liver and promote healing. Minerals such as zinc, selenium, and iron are also important for helping to maintain normal liver function and for fighting off infections.

Fluid intake is also important for people with cirrhosis as it helps to flush toxins and waste from the body. Adequate fluid intake is especially important for people with ascites, which is a condition caused by cirrhosis in which fluid accumulates in the abdomen. Finally, it is important to avoid foods that are high in sodium and saturated fats. Too much sodium can cause fluid retention and can exacerbate the symptoms of cirrhosis. Saturated fats can also increase the risk of developing fatty liver disease, which can worsen cirrhosis.

Nutrition is essential for maintaining health and preventing complications in people with cirrhosis. An adequate calorie intake, adequate vitamins and minerals, adequate fluid intake, and avoiding foods high in sodium and saturated fats are all important considerations for people with cirrhosis. By following these nutritional considerations, people with cirrhosis can help to maintain their overall health and reduce the risk of complications.

CONCLUSION

The vegan Cirrhosis diet cookbook is a great resource for those looking to improve their health and their overall lifestyle. It provides delicious and nutritious recipes that are easy to prepare and follow. The recipes are based on a vegan diet and focus on whole grains, legumes, vegetables, fruits, nuts, and seeds. This cookbook is a great tool for anyone looking to make healthier choices and reduce their risk of chronic diseases such as cirrhosis. The recipes are full of flavor and provide a wide variety of flavors and textures. Whether you are looking to lose weight, improve your health, or just enjoy delicious vegan cooking, the vegan Cirrhosis diet cookbook is a great resource. By following the recipes in the book, you can enjoy tasty, nutritious meals that will help you reach your health goals.